MW01194043

Creating Results That Matter

Creating Results That Matter
A Coaching Manual for Anyone

Dan Kennedy

Creating Results That Matter
by Dan Kennedy

Copyright © 2014 Dan Kennedy. All rights reserved.
Printed in the United States of America.

Editor: Susan Fairo
Cover Design: Becky Pezely
Interior Design and Illustrations: Becky Pezely

Printing History:
July 2014, First Edition.

ISBN: 978-1-4949-8573-8

Contents

Introduction

If you want to learn about coaching and how to use it, welcome. This book is a straight-ahead look at personal coaching and how you can use it to help create results that matter with those who matter to you. Essentially, it's a manual meant to help you to quickly bring coaching into what you already do.

Here you will learn how to have conversations that allow people you're dealing with at work and elsewhere to get clear about what they want and to move toward making it real. Does a shy colleague of yours want to be a better communicator? Is there a mediocre student in your class who's ready to put in the effort to get better grades? Does someone who usually holds back in your congregation want to start a homeless initiative? Using coaching, you can help them create the results that matter to them and do so more intentionally while being more effective and efficient.

Although numerous studies over the years speak to coaching's value both in business and in the personal lives of those who work with a coach,* I'll say up front that I don't think that you need to be a professional coach to coach others. Indeed, I think you'll find that coaching travels well among roles. Managers, co-workers, consultants, mentors, teachers, counselors, pastors, parents and even friends can all have an important influence when they coach. And while you may want to have a more formal coaching relationship with someone—and I'll show you how to do that—I think you'll see that coaching can also blend into

---

* Find out more about the benefits of coaching at the website for the professional body that represents the most coaches, the International Coach Federation: www.CoachFederation.org

more informal conversations. (If you want deeper instruction in coaching I highly recommend that you take courses from any of the many schools accredited by the International Coach Federation. What you'll learn here will be a great foundation for that work.)

You've probably been hearing about non-sports coaching for many years now.[*] I remember living here in Seattle in the late 90's and being stumped. I had been working in tech for over a decade and was ready for a change, but to what, I hadn't a clue. Then, one day I went to my mailbox and found a letter from a friend who lived nearby. I opened the envelope to find that he had clipped and sent me an article from Newsweek magazine on this new field I had never heard of called life coaching. My friend had attached a note that said: "This is kind of what you naturally do, anyway." I read the article and though I thought that the new profession looked interesting, I doubted there was anything like it happening in Seattle and so didn't think much of it. But then, two days later, I went to the mailbox again and found a letter from another pal containing the same clipping and another encouraging note. What a coincidence, I thought. And then, a few days later while I was at a friend's home for dinner, she came out of the kitchen waving a piece of paper saying, "I almost forgot. Here Dan, I've been saving this Newsweek article for you." Okay, now I was paying attention!

Over the next few months I met many coaches both here locally and then from around the country at the first-ever coaching conference, which was held in the Bay Area. By this time I felt that coaching was real and was something I could and wanted to do. I went on to take formal coaching training and then helped form the International Coach Federation's local chapter. Soon, I was coaching executives, entrepreneurs, career-changers and others. In time I began teaching coaching as a leadership skill at various area colleges. (The first versions of this manual were

---

[*]   See Appendix A for a short history of the profession.

created then.) My students were mostly managers, supervisors and consultants, although the University of Wisconsin flew me out to train some of their student leaders how to coach. What a progressive institution!

Along the way I began to see that anyone with the desire and determination to learn coaching could do so without prolonged and formal training. That training was essential for professional coaches, of course, but for anyone who wanted to use a coaching approach in day-to-day interactions, I felt if people could learn the basics and practice on their own, they could see how to use coaching in their daily lives at work and elsewhere.

What I've done in this book is to take a holistic approach. If you want the basics, you'll find them here. But if you want to do more in your coaching you'll not only find instructions on how to coach, but also information on how to prepare the people you coach—your coachees—with exercises that will help them to become more self-aware. That knowledge will offer a powerful way for them to see where they want to go in their lives, what will give them the energy to get there, and how coaching will help along the way. I suggest that you do the exercises yourself for a couple of reasons. First, you'll see what you discover about yourself. And second, you'll be able to better identify with what your coachees will learn when they do them, too.

Something I've noticed is that most people who take my coaching workshops don't practice and learn all the techniques and perspectives that I expose them to. Instead, they try the things that they think will apply to their own situations. Unless you want to be a professional coach or your work dictates that you fully embrace coaching, my guess is that you'll do the same thing. So, go ahead and experiment. The good news is that if you take the time to read this manual and practice even just some of what you find here, you'll change how you relate to others in important, worthwhile and noticeable ways.

My thanks go out to my collaborators on this book: Susan Fairo, my editor, and the book's designer, Becky Pezely. I will always appreciate my first coach, Helen House, for helping me see what's possible, and the folks at The Coaches Training Institute who, in my opinion, offer the gold standard in coach training. And lastly, I send my appreciation to my students and clients from whom I've learned so much.

I wish you well as you read the pages to come and begin applying what you find here in conversations with the important people in your life. When you do, I think you'll discover that coaching will change the both of you for the better.

Dan Kennedy
Seattle, 2014

What is Coaching?

Coaching comes in many flavors. There are life coaches, career coaches, executive and business coaches and more. And other professionals like managers, mentors, counselors and consultants often use coaching in the work they do.* But what is coaching, anyway? There are quite a few definitions out there, but what they all have in common is the fact that coaching is the process of actively engaging a person in creating results that matter to them. It's pretty simple, really, but not easy! The simple part is the fact that coaching rests on just a few concepts and skills. The challenge is in actually learning them, and it's only a problem if you don't take the time or allow yourself to grasp them through trial and error. A sage once said, "Sometimes you win, and sometimes you learn." Practicing your coaching skills lets you do both. Learning coaching is easier when you see its benefits. Here are just a few:

FOR THOSE WHO COACH, IT...

- Saves time for the person coaching by encouraging coachees to take more control and responsibility for what needs to be done.
- Increases productivity in the workplace and elsewhere by decreasing "have to" activity and increasing "want to" proactivity and performance.
- Improves relationships.
- Inspires motivation.

---

* For an intriguing article on the field of coaching as well as its relationship to therapy, see the cover story in the May 2014 issue of Harper's magazine.

FOR THE PERSON BEING COACHED, IT...

- Increases performance, learning and effectiveness.
- Facilitates self-awareness.
- Increases engagement in work and life.

FOR YOUR ORGANIZATION, COACHING...

- Is an excellent return on investment since it leverages training, career development and outplacement dollars.
- Improves attraction rates. More and more, coaching is being seen as something offered to valuable employees.
- Increases retention rates. Coaching keeps employees involved and focused on productive and satisfying activities.
- Supports the growth of "high potentials" as well as those challenged in their professional development.
- Maximizes employee engagement which leads to greater productivity and profitability for the organization, plus higher levels of customer loyalty.

Are you beginning to see how coaching offers value on several levels and can create results that really matter? To coach is to give time, talent and willingness to support someone else. To be coached is to take a significant step towards getting clear about what is important to you and then to actually do something about it. In coaching, two people learn to trust and be trusted and sometimes to do more than either thought possible. Coaching offers something of value from start to finish—for both of you.

To start, we are about to build our foundation and explore coaching's essential concepts. Following that, we'll look at a method that can keep us on track in our coaching conversations so that we, and the people we coach, will get the most from our time together. This will be followed by descriptions of the specific coaching activities and skills that will help you co-create with your coachees the results that matter to them. Along the way you'll see several "Try This" sections that will invite you to actually practice and do what you are reading about. Do try them! It's how you will learn and begin to make coaching yours. So, then, let's begin...

The Essentials

Coaching is built on the basic perspectives that follow. As you read, begin thinking about how you can make them your own.

We are all creative and resourceful

Remember that coaching is a creative process. Some of what you are reading in this manual reflects a style of coaching that is called Co-Active® Coaching.* A key aspect of that approach is the belief that we are all resourceful and creative and as such, we can set our own goals and discover and/or create our own answers. Coaching facilitates that process. Since people can come to their own solutions, a good deal of coaching—and this is important—consists of asking your coachees lots of good questions to unearth those answers, or the strategies to find them.

One of my first clients was Mary Ann, a successful artist from Austin whose work was sold in galleries around the country. She had recently divorced and had decided to move herself and her two boys to Seattle. She felt that a coach could help her make the transition of her business and family a smoother one and we soon started working together.

During one coaching call she said, "Dan, as an artist, I need lots of quiet time to just be with myself. Thing is, with a family plus commitments at my new church and elsewhere, not to mention running my business and actually painting, I'm being pulled every which way and am getting next to no time to myself. Whenever

_____

* Developed by The Coaches Training Institute: www.TheCoaches.com

the kids or other people in my life want my time I forget that sometimes I just need to say no. But I don't and before I know it I'm going off and doing something for anyone who wants me. I dearly need my own time."

I said, "Mary Ann, since downtime is so important to you, let me ask you: What can you do to keep your priority of quiet time top of mind so that whenever and wherever anyone starts making a claim on your schedule, you'll know to say no?" Immediately, I thought of the answer to my own question: If you need to remember to say no then just put sticky notes everywhere with the words "Just Say No!" on them.

Feeling very proud of my instant and to my mind, at least, obvious answer, I was sure she'd come up with it, too, and so I waited. It took a while, but she finally said, "I've got a good idea. At our old home we lived near a creek, and every time I wanted to be alone I would stroll on over to it, take a seat on the bank and just be. Well, just before we all got in the car to drive to Seattle, I took one last walk over to my creek. As I stood there I looked down and saw how the shore was covered in pebbles. I'm not sure why, exactly, but I bent down and picked up a handful of them and brought them with us here to our new home. Well, I'm always wearing jeans, so I think that every day I'm going to remind myself how important my quiet time is by putting one of those small stones in my pocket. That way I'll always feel it and remember what's most important so when someone asks me for a favor, I'll take a moment to think about if it is really a good idea or not, and if not, then I'll just say no."

"By not knowing as the coach we clear the way for the coachee to claim their own goals, and find their own paths."

– Anonymous

I couldn't have made that answer up! It was her perfect answer for her. If I had immediately told her about the sticky notes she may have never taken the time to come up with her own answer to the question. And her answer was better than mine because it was hers and so she'd be more likely to do it. Lesson learned: Ask questions and believe that the coachee is creative and resourceful and can come up with her own solution.

You're both learning

The belief that our coachees have or can find their own answers presents people who coach the largest of challenges: keeping their opinions to themselves! This includes the need for a dash of humility because when we coach, we need to be open to learning along with our coachees; we can't go in thinking we will help, fix or rescue the people with our own solutions. Several negative consequences can flow from our being seen as a regular source of advice:

> "In the beginner's mind there are many possibilities. In the expert's there are few."
> – Shunryu Suzuki

- If what we suggest works, the coachee cannot take credit for the results and confidence can suffer.
- If we are wrong, we get the blame and trust is damaged.
- People may feel they have to do what we say by virtue of our position—as the one coaching, if nothing else. Feeling forced leads to lower energy and enthusiasm.
- Coachees may feel they are limited to just discussing issues that we're experts on and, as a result, feel constrained. However, we can actually coach about almost anything, no matter how little or how much we know about it.
- There is nearly always more than one way to do things. Coachees may do it your way when their way might have better results, and certainly would be a better learning experience.

- People learn less effectively when told the answers.
- If we are often seen as the source of answers, we will be unwittingly training people to be reliant on us and not to think and risk for themselves. (And with this reputation, chances are, you'll be spending more and more of your time solving everyone's problems.)

So, put your answers away. Go ahead and be curious, ask questions and allow yourself to be pleasantly surprised.

The coachee takes responsibility

An important companion to the idea that your coachees can come up with their own answers is that, especially in a more formal coaching relationship, they own the process and the results of their coaching. After all, they step up and ask you for some coaching—or accept your offer to do it—plus they figure out along the way what to do to get where they decide to go. And then, of course, they actually do it. It's all theirs.

Coaching is collaborative

By now you may be starting to see that coaching is a collaborative process. If you have some authority over someone, it may not be unusual for you to tell them what to do. But whether you are in charge or not, or you're the expert or not, when you coach, you and the person you're coaching are peers in the process of discovery.

"Good coaches will coach beyond the limits of their knowledge."

– John Whitmore

The difference is action

Coachees take on a lot of responsibility, from determining the coaching topic du jour to discovering their own answers. But it doesn't end there. Most coaching conversations would normally be like other incredibly interesting discussions if not for one thing: Coaching results in a commitment to action. The coachee commits to acting in their best behalf, and soon. It's about performance.

Engagement is vital

Remember that coaching engages people in creating the results that matter to them. "Engages" is a key term, here. After all, coachees ask for or accept the coaching, then they consider the powerful questions posed by the person coaching them. They also take responsibility for their own answers and along the way they are called upon to be creative and resourceful. And to top it all off, they need to stretch and act on their own behalf. This is how coaching draws people into their work and lives like never before, and supports them in creating the results they want in powerful ways. A coaching conversation engages people like no other.

It all depends on trust and caring

Finally, we come to trust and caring—if any two ideas fuel the rest, it's these. When coaching, you must trust the people you are working with. Trust them to be truthful, and trust that they will follow-through on what they say they will do. In other words, trust your coachee to be honest and to have integrity. Trust that they can do what must be done—show confidence in them. This goes both ways, of course and they will need to trust you. Are you trustworthy? Can you hold your discussions with each other in confidence, and do they feel you have their best

"Perhaps the greatest benefit the coach brings to the conversation is to trust clients more than the clients trust themselves . . . The most important thing is that the care be there. The coach has to care about the person being coached and the person needs to know it."

- Timothy Gallwey

interests at heart? Do you care? Do they know it? How?

Whom and when to coach

So, when and where should you think about doing some coaching?
The best and the not quite right scenarios for coaching each have
their own characteristics.

Coaching works well when:

- The person to be coached wants to accomplish something
  and is open to stretching and learning along the way.
- You both have a good relationship.
- You both are willing to engage in coaching.
- The person has proven coachable, e.g., has a history of
  keeping their word.
- If you are coaching a co-worker, the organization has a
  coaching culture that supports risk, failure and learning.

It won't work as well when:

- Your relationship with the other person is poor.
- The person fulfills the minimal requirements of their work.
- There is a history of power struggles between you.
- The person refuses coaching.
- The organizational culture is non-empowering.
- Time is of the essence and decisions and actions need to
  happen soon.

All that said, don't completely dismiss coaching for people you
have doubts about. They may have never experienced its power.
Use your judgment and with their permission, try it where you
both see some possibilities.

I've been asked on several occasions to work with abrasive
managers, people who inflict psychological trauma on their
employees with their unnecessary roughness. At first, you'd

think that these folks wouldn't be open to coaching; often they think they are doing a good job and don't see what all the fuss is about. And they don't ask for a coach; they are given a coach, i.e. me. But after a Co-360 Assessment (Appendix C) they finally get that their impact is really hurting people, and it's then that they're usually up for trying to change, and often they do. So, be open and allow whomever you might coach to think about it. They may be more ready than you know.

GROW: Pointing the Way

When I was first getting into coaching, things felt squishy to me. Here I was, learning about its essential concepts and skills, but I wondered how I would fit them into a real coaching conversation. I wanted at least a bit of structure along the way and to know where my clients and I would be heading together. I wanted a road map. Then, I discovered GROW.

GROW is an acronym developed by master coach, John Whitmore, and others to help direct the flow of a coaching conversation.[*] The letters stand for: Goal, Reality, Options and Willingness. Let's look at each one separately.[**]

Goal

The result that matters to the coachee. It can be about a distant accomplishment, or as simple and near as the goal of that day's coaching session. For a challenging or distant goal, this is the best time to explore what the coachee hopes to gain as a result of reaching it. In other words, ask about the motivation behind the goal. You want to help a person to get clear about the benefits of their goal to build up the momentum they will need to pursue it later on when the going might get tough.

> "You get the best effort from others not by lighting a fire beneath them, but by building a fire within."
>
> - Bob Nelson

---

[*] John Whitmore, Coaching for Performance: GROWing human potential and purpose. (London, Nicholas Brealey, 2006)

[**] Appendix B contains many good GROW questions.

Here are a few questions for the Goal phase of your conversation, starting with the most important coaching question of all:

- What do you want?
- How come?
- Is this a primary or secondary goal?

Reality

Before moving toward the person's goal, it's good to examine the facts and assumptions that surround it—the reality of the situation. Ask about things like: what's been tried so far, who has been involved in the past and who might be in the future, time and budget realities, etc. If you and your coachee have feedback about themselves from a 360-degree assessment, that can be an excellent source for determining some of the reality of the situation, as well.*

> "I am able to control only that which I am aware of. That which I am unaware of controls me. Awareness empowers me."
>
> - John Whitmore

Examining the person's assumptions about all of this is an essential thing to do at this point since they determine how he views the goal and what can be done to reach it. One of the most important things about thoroughly examining the reality of the situation is that often, just by thinking and talking about it, a person will discover new approaches and insights that wouldn't have come up if you both hadn't had the conversation.

Some Reality questions:

- What have you done so far?
- What can you control here? Influence? Have you no control over?
- What is the risk?

---

* An easy-to-use 360 assessment is in Appendix C.

Options

Now your conversation begins to tilt towards the coachee actually doing something. It is time to generate possibilities. If your coachee is having problems doing so try brainstorming or mind-mapping, which we'll cover soon. Once some options are generated then help them to choose the best one(s).

A few Options questions:

- What are your options here?
- Imagine that you have what you want. How did you get it?
- Would you like to try some brainstorming?

Willingness

Now, the coaching conversation most clearly becomes different from any other. Here is where you ask for a commitment to action and find out what the coachee is willing to do and by when, and also how the person will let you know that the action has been performed.

Willingness questions can include:

- What are you going to do?
- By when?
- How can you let me know that you did it?

> "Circumstances don't alter commitments;
> commitments alter circumstances."
>
> - Robert Fritz

The Arc

I often picture a coaching conversation looking like an arc, with a fixed start and ending and everything in-between. When I'm coaching and want to remember the GROW model I always think of an image like this one:

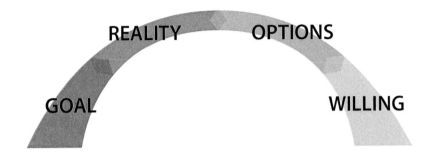

Illustration 1. The arc of a coaching conversation

The arc of that conversation won't always take the left-to-right GROW trajectory. Sliding back and forth in the GROW model isn't unusual. Also, if your present conversation builds on a previous one that already covered some of the GROW territory, you can lightly review or entirely pass over what you've already discussed. And don't get locked into the model. Go where you need to go at the moment to serve the other person.

Try This: Coach Yourself

Let's do a little self-coaching. Take 10-15 minutes and work your way through the GROW model with yourself as your client. If you like, set up two chairs across from each other. When you are playing coach, sit and speak from one chair and when you respond as yourself, sit in the other one.

Pick something you want to create that's either a big deal or a not so big one. The idea is to practice. Talk your way through the process, asking questions as coach and answering them as yourself as the client. This is not only a great way to practice, but it's a valuable way to talk with yourself in a way that will help you get clarity and to achieve more in your life.

Key Activities and Skills

Next up are things to do as you move forward in the coaching relationship and in your actual coaching.

Get permission

As you may have gathered by now, coaching is a voluntary process and involves trust between the two of you. And it can happen anytime, anywhere. With practice, there'll be times that you can naturally move into a coaching conversation with someone without calling attention to the fact you're doing so. Still, it's such an intentional and different way of communicating that usually, you'll want to be sure that the person does, indeed, want to be coached so that they're really on board.

Feel free to bring coaching up with someone you think would benefit from it by saying something like, "Would you like some coaching about that?" If they ask what you mean by coaching, you can say, "This situation sounds like it's a challenge for you. If you like, I'll just ask you a few questions to help you get more clarity about what you want and how you'll make it happen. What do you say?" And they'll go for it or not.

Design the partnership

If you think you'll usually have the more informal kind of coaching interactions, you can skip this section and move on to the section called: Be curious. Otherwise, if you are going to have a formal and ongoing connection with someone for their development over time, you will want to design your alliance together. Here is what you will want to cover in an intake meeting to create your partnership:

COACHING OVERVIEW

Here at the start is the perfect time to talk with your coachee about the coaching concepts discussed in The Essentials chapter above as well as any of the ideas in the pages to come that you think will apply. Make sure you both understand how they will play a part in your work together.

SCOPE

At this point, you both want to decide on the scope of the coaching—will it only revolve around work issues, for example. Specific goals are defined at this stage, as well.

VALUES, STRENGTHS AND PURPOSE

It is also good if you can help your coachees to clarify their values, strengths and purpose for their lives. Values are a person's key motivators, strengths are their natural talents, and life purpose gives direction to one's professional and personal lives. These are powerful reference points for making decisions about where and how to spend one's energy and time moving forward. Appendices D and E include exercises for identifying values and purpose. An exploration of strengths along with an assessment is found in the book, StrengthsFinder 2.0, by Tom Rath. (Or go to www.gallupstrengthscenter.com.) Values, strengths and purpose are all things the coachee can begin working on immediately and can sometimes take a week or two to complete.

STRUCTURE

Decide logistics: where you'll meet, how long and how often, if you'll usually talk in person or by phone, plus how to deal with cancellations.

Allow plenty of time for all of this for, if all goes well, you will both come out of it not only with more clarity about what your partnership will look like, but also with a greater appreciation of and trust for each other.

Be curious

Curiosity serves you well in all phases of a coaching conversation. You'll want to be curious about that day's coaching agenda, the coachee's goals, motivations, assumptions, and solutions. Curious about what he or she will actually do to get the results they want. People who coach want to know. They wonder about their coachees. They ask. They probe. They rummage around the data and options. They are detectives after clues, hounds sniffing tracks, reporters following leads. They want to know. Curiosity serves both parties well.

The most powerful questions that curious coaches ask are the open-ended ones. Good open-ended questions often begin with "Who," "What," "When," "Where," or "How." (Appendix B has a list of powerful questions based on the GROW model.) Such questions lead to more exploration, introspection, clarification, analysis, awareness and learning. Questions with answers that throw up a roadblock with a simple "yes" or "no," aren't nearly as rich. That is why those kinds of questions are called closed-ended.

"Mostly it's the dumb, elementary questions followed up by a dozen even more elementary questions that yield the pay dirt."

- Tom Peters

To prove the rule, there is one open-ended question I recommend you not ask often, if at all, and that is, "Why did you do that?" Asking that can cause a person to want to defend their actions or focus too much on the past. In coaching, we focus on helping the coachee move from now into the future.

Remember that coaching "engages" people in creating results that matter to them. Asking questions—the more powerful the better—keeps people engaged.

Try This: Be Curious

Today, be a bit more curious than usual in your interactions with others. Ask more open-ended questions, give less advice and see where your conversations go. What happens when you ask open-ended questions versus closed-ended ones? Experiment. How are these conversations different?

Focus

Sometimes coachees will come to sessions brimming with issues to talk about. You can't deal with all the topics at once, so ask them to choose (focus on) one to start with and if you have time later, you can move on to the next one.

Bottom-line it

There are times when exploring means finding the short route! This shows up in coaching when the coachee is relating a story that has a conclusion that is relevant, but is on the far side of a long tale. Since you might be in a situation where you need to make the most of your limited coaching time, tell the person so and then ask him her to "bottom-line" the story: to get to the point or the lesson learned.

Use inquiries

On the other side of the time spectrum, sometimes you may want to leave a coachee with an open-ended question to ponder for a few days. This kind of question is known as an inquiry and can be a rich source for insight. An inquiry doesn't necessarily have one answer. Some examples:

- "What are you tolerating?"
- "If you knew you couldn't fail, what would you do here?"
- "What don't you know?"
- "What is there to be grateful for here?"

Listen

By now I hope you're beginning to see the value of you listening more than talking. When your coachees respond to your questions and observations they are actively engaged in working things out. Give them the time and attention to do this. The more they talk (and you listen) the more likely it is that they'll get clearer about what they need to know and do next. Keep your talking-to-listening ratio to at least one-to-five.

Also, notice if you're doing reflective or reactive listening. In reflective listening you are truly considering what is being said, so much so that you can easily repeat it back to the speaker, which is a good thing to do fairly regularly. Reactive listening, on the other hand, is merely you waiting to insert your opinion or solution into the conversation.

"We learn more by looking for the answer to a question and not finding it than we do from learning the answer itself."

- Lloyd Alexander

Finally, try to notice during the coaching when you're going off on mental tangents, like: "My sister had a problem like that once.

I should call her tonight . . ." And off we go, leaving the coachee, not to mention the entire conversation, in our mental dust. Stay with the coachee and listen. It's good for both of you.

Try This: Pay Attention

In the next conversation you have today make a point of noticing—Are you listening reflectively or reactively? How much are you really staying with the other person and how much is your mind wandering off to something else? And either way, how does it affect what's said? Of course, if you can, do this review <u>after</u> your conversation!

Share

As you listen you will notice that there are lots of ways that you can respond. In all cases, what you share needs to be non-evaluative. The purpose of sharing is to raise the coachee's awareness and then to let them react however they will. The best sharing is sparked by what you notice regarding relevant circumstances and behavior. When sharing, always ask permission to do so first, to keep control more in the hands of the coachee. Also, do not be too attached to what you share. Let the person you are coaching know that what you are saying is meant to clarify the situation and that if you aren't accurate, he or she should let you know. Some kinds of sharing include:

OFFERING NEW FACTS

Sometimes you know something that your coachee doesn't and may be important. "Jim, that's a great goal you have for your department, but I think it's time to tell you that you are in line for a promotion that will be taking you to a new part of the company within the month, if you go for it."

NOTICING

Noticing assumptions that the coachee seems to be making. "Nicole, you seem to be acting as though no one will support you on this project."

REFLECTING

Verbally reflecting what the coachee has just said (while listening reflectively as discussed above). By doing so, the coachee then gets to hear what he or she just expressed and can react to it. "Joanne, what I hear you saying is that you want children someday and that you're not sure what effect that will have on your career."

INTUITION

If you feel something to be true, share it with your coachee and see how it "lands." "Bill, I have a hunch that you really don't want to be working on this. What do you think?"

OBSERVATIONS

Observations can be offered as long as it is clear to both of you that they contain no judgment: "Mary, I've noticed that even though graphic design isn't a part of your job description, you seem to put a lot of artistic energy into every proposal we send out."

TRUTH-TELLING

Here you share what you see, even if it isn't pretty: "Mark, you've promised to get those reports in every week for the last month, but you haven't even started them. It seems that you don't really care."

ADVICE

Advice is at the bottom of this list about sharing for a reason! As we've said, coaching is simple, but not easy, and it is here that we face our toughest challenge in coaching: not telling people what to do or giving them our answer. This can be tough since we often have expertise to offer. What good is it if we can't share it? For the answer, refer back to the section "You're both learning" on page 17.

"People tolerate your ideas, but they act on their own."

- Randall Root

It isn't that expertise has no value, it's just that it is of less value when you are coaching. The less you know about the topic at hand, the more curious you will be and the more powerful questions you will ask. All that said, however, there are a couple of situations in which you should consider offering advice.

One is when time is short, such as a deadline being an hour away. Another is when the coachee is truly stumped and can't possibly come up with anymore ideas. (In each case, though, be sure that you first have the coachee's permission to give your advice—remember, it's still their show.)

"We are more easily persuaded, in general, by the reasons we ourselves discover, than by those which are given to us by others."

- Blaise Pascal

Encourage

I assume that you believe in those you coach along with their abilities. What's interesting is that sometimes, you'll believe in them more than they do themselves. So, encourage them to act in their best behalf. Praise them when they do, and always acknowledge their effort and the kind of person they are needing to be to move forward.* Try making it a habit to offer this sincere acknowledgment at the end of every coaching session. It's a wonderful way to end the conversation.

> "Praise, like gold and diamonds,
> owes its value to its scarcity."
>
> - Samuel Johnson

---

* For more, see: Heidie Grant Halvorson, Ph.D. Succeed: How We Can Reach Our Goals (London, Plume, 2010)

Promoting Action

Promoting action definitely belongs in the list of Key Activities and Skills above, but there's enough to say about it that it deserves its own chapter. Since coaching is about creating results that matter, actions need to take place to do that creating. As a pastor I once trained said, "Coaching gives me tools for my ministry to help those I serve to stop spinning their wheels and to actually move forward on their journeys." Below are a series of tools for creating action steps, and ways to make sure there's follow-through.

Creating action steps

Sometimes, the challenge to achieving goals is coming up with things to do to reach them. When the coachee runs out of ideas or has none to begin with, ask her to try either or both of these time-tested techniques for generating some more:

BRAINSTORMING

As you probably know, this is a form of idea generation that has an "anything goes" phase that includes both of you sharing any ideas that come up around a topic, then a more realistic phase where the more practical options are chosen for further consideration. By the way, do not offer to brainstorm with your coachees as a round-about way of exposing them to your solutions. One way to guard against this is to only suggest brainstorming when you yourself have at least two ideas to contribute.

MIND-MAPPING

A graphic and free-form way to generate ideas and options. This is done by drawing a circle on a page and writing inside of it the name of the issue or topic at hand. Then, new circles representing any related concepts or activities are drawn and labeled, each circle branching off from the original and connected to it with a line. As new ideas come up, more circles can then be drawn based on the ones that came before, and so on. Later, all the ideas can be put in a list or outline form. The point is to let ideas flow and show up anywhere on the page. This is especially useful for people who are visual thinkers.

STRETCHING

By the way, if you feel your coachee could do more than what they say they are willing to do, go ahead and challenge them with a stretch goal. Remember, however, that with all your requests, the coachee can either accept it, say "no" to it, or make a counter-offer. I remember talking with my own coach once about going for a run three days a week to help me keep fit. She suggested that I run five; I countered with four and four it was.

Ensuring follow-through

Resistance to taking that next step can be powerful and it comes in several guises, like procrastination, rationalization and just plain fear. Here are some ways to make sure that the person you're coaching does what needs to be done:

PURPOSE-PLOTTING, VALUES-SPOTTING AND STRENGTH-FINDING

Common sense and current research both say that the more we care about a goal, the greater the chance of a successful outcome.[*]

---

[*] For an extensive and well-researched book about how to see the world in a way that allows us to tap all of our resources to succeed, read: Shawn Achor, Before Happiness: The 5 Hidden Keys to Achieving Success, Spreading Happiness, and

Knowing who we are—our purpose, values and strengths—helps us choose goals that matter to us. We have covered this before but as a review, our life's purpose is our own true north—the direction we want our lives to take. Meanwhile, values have been called the emotional paycheck of work, and they are really the emotional underpinnings to all we do. Use the exercises in the Appendices to help you identify your coachee's (not to mention your own) purpose and values and don't forget to use the StrengthsFinder 2.0 book or online assessment mentioned earlier to uncover strengths. Appeal to your coachee's purpose, values and strengths when they seem lost or unwilling to act.

PUTTING IN THE EFFORT

And other research points out that we're more likely to achieve a goal when we put in real effort that includes planning, persistence and developing good strategies.[*] Here are some tips to share with your coachees to help them increase their chances of success:

- Be specific about what you want to create so you have a clear idea about what success looks like. Planning to run three miles every weekday is better than saying you'll be sure to run more.

> "No matter your ability, effort is what ignites that ability and turns it into accomplishment."
> - Carol Dweck

- Decide what you will do in advance. So, the next time your co-worker makes one of their snide comments about your performance in a meeting, thinking they are being funny, promise yourself that you'll take them aside immediately afterwards and tell them that you don't appreciate it.
- Focus on what you will do, not on what you won't. Instead

Sustaining Positive Change (New York, Crown Business, 2013)

[*] See: Carol Dweck, Ph.D., Mindset: The New Psychology of Success (New York, Ballantine Books, 2006)

of trying not to overly criticize your people at work, focus on encouraging them and asking how you can support their success.

REFRAMING

Helping the coachee to get a new perspective on a situation can often turn things around. For example, what if the person has committed to getting ready for an upcoming marathon and needs to run every day, rain or shine, and rain is likely for most of the days leading up to the event? And what if cold, rainy days are just not that person's cup of tea? If it looks like weather could get in the way of training, ask the coachee for three other ways to see—to reframe—the situation. One perspective could be that if on race day it's raining, the person will be ready for it.

Now, let's look at fear. Fear is a big topic, of course, and helping those we coach to reframe how they see it is a powerful way to help them follow-through on their commitments. Many books have been written about fear but coach and author, Rich Fettke, takes a useful approach to it which he calls our Protector. He suggests that we engage it as a teacher, spend time with it, and ask what it wants us to do before or as we move forward.*

> "Whenever any form of fear arises, turn toward it with affection, thank it silently in your mind, and watch what happens."
>
> - Richard Schaub

For instance, if a coachee is hesitating to take on a challenging new project at work because she's afraid of failing and looking the fool, you, as her coach could ask her if her Protector is at work. If she says yes, you could ask her to invite her Protector into the conversation, i.e., to notice where it is showing up as a

---

* Rich Fettke, Extreme Success: The 7-Part Program That Shows You How to Succeed Without Struggle (New York, Fireside, 2002)

feeling in her body, and then to breathe and then ask it what it wants her to know before she moves forward. It may be saying, for example, that she needs to do more research about the project or to enlist a collaborator before going further. The idea is to see what normally would stop someone as actually being something else—in this case, as a resource that is asking her to slow down, perhaps, but not to stop.

CHUNKING DOWN

When a task seems overwhelming due to its complexity or how much needs to be done, have the coachee chunk it down and break the task into smaller steps. Then, ask him or her to do only one or two of the steps by your next session.

COMPELLING CONSEQUENCES

Here, a situation is created where something very real is at stake if the person doesn't follow through. The consequences must be important, immediate and allow for no fudging—either it was done or it was not. For example, your coachee checks his Facebook page so much at work that he's starting to miss important deadlines. The next time he misses one he promises to immediately tell his boss that he's volunteering to lead their next team meeting, which is something he hates doing. This is a tool to use when resistance is high and the person you're coaching is willing. In fact, let them come up with the consequences themselves and then ask why they are so compelling.

WINS

When the person you're coaching has doubts about being able to take the next step, have them write down a list of three instances when they've succeeded in similar situations in the past. By doing so the task ahead will seem all the more possible.

Solving Problems vs. Creating Results

This is probably a good place to address the fact that coaching is not about solving people's problems. Surprising, yes?

Don't dwell in the problems

Remember that the focus of coaching is creating results that matter. Any problem solving, then, is but a stepping-stone on the way to reaching a specified destination: the result or goal, as defined by the coachee. Solving problems is different than creating results in several ways:

Problem Solving	Creating Results That Matter
Eliminating	Revealing
Reactive	Proactive
Noticing what's wrong	Seeing possibilities
Getting past	Moving into
Efficiency	Growth
Self-centered	Other-centered
Short-term	Longer-term
Answer-oriented	Process-oriented
Oppositional	Relational
Depleting	Energizing

It isn't that problems shouldn't be given attention. In fact, a problem will often be the reason a coaching session takes place. In the GROW model, the problem will usually show up while you are exploring the reality of the situation. After all, reality can include obstacles to getting what we want, like with the artist Mary Ann mentioned above whose problem was not having enough quiet time in her day. Remember that it's the pull of the goal that will lend energy to dealing with problems. For her, her goal and her reason to beat the problem was to find the time to rejuvenate her creativity. So go ahead and look at a problem, but at some point, be sure that the coachee recalls what the goal is that lies beyond it.

Coach the coachee, not the problem

You need to be sure that you are always coaching individuals and not their problems. Remember, we believe that the coachee is creative and resourceful and can almost always come to their own solution. As soon as we get drawn into trying to fix their problems, we leave the coaching role and turn into a consultant at best and a meddler at worst. Refer back to the section "You're both learning" on page 17 for the reasons we don't want to go there.

> "Problem solving is taking action to have something go away—the problem. Creating is taking action to have something come into being—the creation. The greatest leaders and statesmen in history have not been problem solvers. They have been builders."
>
> - Robert Fritz

So, what do we do when confronted with the coachee's challenges? Focus on the coachee, and be curious. Ask yourself where you are in the GROW conversation. What new question can you ask to remind the person why they want to pursue what is on the other side of the problem? (Goal.) What new facts have yet to be discussed? (Reality.) What other options are there? (Options.) What is the coachee really committed to do next to change things? (Willing.)

If you think about it, coaching the individual versus the problem is freeing for you and more valuable for them. You get to focus on the person and to be curious about what they'll do next, and they get to own their answers. This is also why you don't need to have a background in whatever the person wants to talk about. As a coach, you don't need to be a subject-matter expert. In fact, the less you know about the topic at hand the fresher your perspective and questions will be.

What real empowerment looks like

We often feel like we add value to people or an organization if we can solve their problems for them. We also think that it makes us look good. Coaching allows you to take problem solving to a whole new level because with coaching you assist others to be the source of their own answers. In a sense, you give away the glory of being the Answer Man or Woman, and let others get the credit. In that way, coaching offers you a unique way to help people build their confidence and resources—to truly empower them and help them grow.

"Sometimes you win and sometimes you learn."

- Robert Kiyosaki

Try This: Practice Coaching

Now that you've read much of Creating Results That Matter, it's time to try this thing called coaching. Start by identifying your first potential coachee. It should be a friend or co-worker you can trust and with whom you can make mistakes and learn. Let the person know that you are practicing a new skill and would like their help. Make no promises, but let them know you want to work with them to achieve something that's important to them.

I suggest you both plan on several sessions lasting 20-30 minutes each and spaced several days apart, giving the coachee time to accomplish what they commit to doing at each session. Make it work for you and each person you coach. When you ask them for their help, let them know that your times together can be in person or over the phone. Phones are a great way to coach, by the way. Besides being convenient, coaching over the phone can be very effective since those conversations contain only two things: content and emotion—the essence of any good interaction.

Before each call or meeting, decide which skills you will want to practice. But don't box yourself in and only do those. If you need to try other approaches, go for it. At the end of each conversation, be sure to ask your coachee for feedback. Two good questions are: What would you have liked to have seen more of from me? And less of? This can be a great way to practice, learn and build even better relationships with anyone you coach.

Repeat this process with as many people as you like while using more and more of what you are reading about here. In time, not only will you want to have more intentional coaching conversations, but you may well notice that your everyday interactions with others are naturally shifting and taking on more of a coaching "feel."

Conclusion

Somewhere along the line, someone has come up with another acronym—this one to describe the perfect goal or result. It's a SMART one and should be:

- **S**pecific, so it can act as a good target.
- **M**easurable, so ongoing progress can be determined.
- **A**greed upon, so all parties will be singing from the same page along the way.
- **R**ealistic, so it actually can happen, and
- **T**imed, so a deadline is set.

I like the idea of SMART and only quibble with one of the points: Realistic. Part of what coaching can achieve is breaking through what people think is realistic, sensible, or doable. Often we only choose goals that we know can be accomplished. They're relatively safe. While this attitude can be productive, it is also limiting. I suggest that you challenge yourself to challenge your coachees to imagine the goals they would set if they knew they couldn't fail. Make sure they are creating results that matter— results that are worthy of them, and that they really want. If they should fall short, they'll still probably have gone farther than they would have otherwise and will learn a lot along the way.

Which brings us to you. What are your dreams and aspirations? Take a look at your own goals. What results matter to you? The key word here is "matter." Results that matter are what help create the juice, the engagement, the doing, and the learning. When you begin to create results that matter for yourself, you'll know it can happen for others. Is it time to think about a coach for yourself? Besides moving you towards what's important for you, having a coach can help you coach others. You can actually learn to coach better by having a coach of your own.

In the old days, a coach was something—like a stagecoach—that took important people from one place to another. Where do you want to travel next in your life? Choose where you want to go, and if need be, ask a modern-day coach to join you for the ride! You see, coaching can take you, as well as the people you coach, to places you've never seen before and yes, to results that really matter.

Try This: Meet Some Coaches

Attend a meeting of your local chapter of the International Coach Federation. The ICF is the primary credentialing authority for the coaching profession. Chapters usually have regular meetings with presentations and invite the public to attend. While there, be curious about what you can learn about coaching. And if you're in the market for a coach for yourself or your organization, what better place to find one?

Appendices

Appendix A: Coaching's Backstory

Although professional coaching has been going on for decades, coaching only began to crystallize as a real and unique approach in the late 1970s. A key player in the creation of non-sports coaching as a discipline, ironically, was a tennis coach. In 1975, The Inner Game of Tennis, written by a former tennis champion and coach named Timothy Gallwey, showed the world a radical approach to helping people learn. Instead of barking orders or even making suggestions, like most coaches of his day, Gallwey based his method on the belief in the innate ability of people's bodies to learn through experience, and observation. He also helped his students see how their minds could get in their way and be as formidable as the opponent on the other side of the net.

He saw the coach's role as one of asking powerful questions that would help players to increase their awareness of how they played and how they thought, and to adjust accordingly. Gallwey believed that the game of tennis, like the game of life, was one of expressing our potential and being the source of our own answers.

Many of those who came to learn the Inner Game were business people. They soon saw that this new message they were hearing on the court could be applied in their boardrooms, as well. It was obvious that this coaching style could help manager/leaders assist their people to take better control of their jobs and careers, and to get results that were rare in the command-and-control management culture of the day. In time, Inner Game coaches found themselves literally going to work across America to spread the word. Meanwhile, a student of Gallwey's named John Whitmore was bringing the Inner Game to Europe. At the same time, well known sports coaches were being hired to speak to employees in many American companies, further helping to blend the concepts of coaching, management, and leadership.

By the start of the 1990's other pioneers were taking steps to bring coaching to new levels of acceptance and professionalism. Some of those contributors included Thomas Leonard, a former financial planner who founded the coach training company, Coach U. Around the same time, a colleague of Leonard's and a former CPA and auditor, Laura Whitworth, along with Henry Kimsey-House, a career development professional, began The Coaches Training Institute. Today, dozens of schools are devoted to training people to become professional coaches.

In 1998 the Professional & Personal Coaches Association (PPCA) and The International Coach Federation (ICF) joined together to create the primary body representing and supporting professional coaches today. (The ICF name remains.) Soon thereafter the ICF took the next step in professional development by starting to offer certification to coaches who qualify. Since then the ICF has created a definition for professional coaching and educates the public about how it compares with other key services like therapy and consulting.

Today, companies routinely hire coaches (or train their own) to assist managers with everything from professional and leadership development to process improvement.[*] Some savvy

---

[*]   In 2012 an extensive study by the Conference Board found that coaching continues to grow in corporate settings. Go to www.conference-board.org and search for the coaching survey. For a comprehensive overview about coaching and how it is being implemented in organizations, read: Managing Coaching at Work: Developing, Evaluating and Sustaining Coaching in Organizations, Jackie Keddy

organizations are even using coaching as a perk to attract and retain key contributors. Meanwhile, individuals regularly hire coaches to help them with career, business and personal growth goals. The demand is there. In fact, at last count there were 50,000 people calling themselves coaches. If it hasn't been clear for all these years, it certainly is now: coaching is here to stay.

and Clive Johnson. (London, Kogan Page, 2011)

Appendix B: Powerful Questions Based on GROW

GOAL:
- What do you want? What results matter to you?
- What do you want to get out of this session?
- Is this a primary or secondary goal?
- Of all the issues you've brought up here, which would you like to look at first?
- Why is that goal of value to you?
- What are some good reasons for achieving it?
- Who would benefit from this goal besides you?
- You say that you want to solve a problem. What is it in the way of? What's on the other side of it that's worth pursuing?
- How does what you want fit into the bigger picture?

REALITY:
- What do you already know about this?
- What does it mean to you?
- What don't you know?
- What are you not paying attention to?
- What have you done so far? What results did that produce?
- What can you control here? Influence? Have you no control over?
- I'm picking up some fear here. Does your Protector have anything to say?
- What are you avoiding doing that you know needs to be done?
- Where is the risk?
- What will be the impact of getting what you want? On yourself? On others?
- What would need to happen for you to let go of this goal?
- What assumptions are you making? What makes them true?
- What is another perspective you could have about this?

- What would be the costs of not doing this?
- Who is involved? What would their perspective be about this?
- Have you ever been in a similar situation? How did you handle it?
- How does this fit into the larger picture?
- What are your obstacles, both internal and external?
- What resources are available?
- What books, websites, classes or experts could you learn from about this?

OPTIONS:

- What are all your options?
- What are some different ways you can come at this?
- What else could you do?
- What would you do if you could start over?
- What if there were no constraints and you weren't being realistic?
- How would you do this if you knew you couldn't fail?
- Imagine you now have what you want. Retrace your steps. How did you get it?
- Would you like to brainstorm or make a mind-map?
- Would you like another idea?
- What are the pluses and minuses of each choice?
- Which one(s) do you choose?
- Who could help you?
- Who needs to be involved? How will you get their buy-in?
- What problems could you encounter? How could you be ready for them?
- What would you do if you were courageous?

WILLING:

- Which option do you choose?
- What will you do? By when? How will I know you did it?
- How can you "chunk it down" into more manageable steps?

- How will you know you are successful?
- How can someone else or I support you?
- On a scale of 1-10, how strong is your commitment to doing this?
- What would need to happen to raise that score?

Appendix C: The Co-360 Assessment and Review[SM]

The Co-360° Personal Assessment and Review is a collaborative process that gives valuable feedback to an employee from others in their workplace that the person can then use to make significant changes in their behavior. It's simple, affordable, and effective. Here is how it works:

The employee and their manager, plus you as the employee's coach, co-create questions that will be asked of the significant people in the employee's professional circle. The three of you will design the questions to uncover information that will help the coachee develop. Although most of the questions will be open-ended to elicit the richest responses, it is also a good idea to ask for ratings, like, "On a scale of 1-10 where 10 is very satisfied, what score do you give Rick as a leader?"

The list of people you will be contacting will also be created by the three of you. After they are told that you will be in touch with them you then call or meet with all the contacts and ask them the questions and record their answers. (Those whom you speak with are assured of anonymity, in that no specific feedback will be attributed to anyone in particular.) You then write a report based on your findings.

The report can be a simple summary of the answers to each of the questions, with your relevant feedback and suggestions at the end. The employee and manager get the report, and you and the coachee then have an excellent document from which the employee can get a better handle on the reality of what they are dealing with on the job plus what they might want to do about it.

Either when the coaching is winding down or at a predetermined time while coaching is in full swing, it's a good idea to go back and ask the same people the same questions to see how the coachee has progressed.

Appendix D: Instructions for Spotting Your Values

Values explain why we do what we do and are our underlying motivations. They are internal; we probably learned them when we were quite young. We each have dozens or more values. Values can be sparked in us by certain externals like other people, or money or things, but ultimately, our values are inside of us. Some would say our values <u>are</u> us. (When we hear advice like, "Just be yourself," it simply means that we should act in accordance with our values.) Certainly, our own unique mix of values makes each of us very special. Discovering our strongest ones is not only invaluable, but relatively easy to do, as we'll see.

"Values are the emotional paycheck of work."

- Howard Figler

Knowing our values benefit us because:

- They help us understand what is special about ourselves, as well as others.
- Knowing our values helps us make deliberate and energizing choices that will engage those values. Choices about which activities to take on as well as what kind of people we spend time with can all be made using our values as a guide.
- And if we pursue our goals doing what inspires our values, the process of moving forward will be all the more easy and enjoyable.

Values are easy to spot. Here are some simple ways to do it:

EXERCISE 1: FLIP IT

Think of things that frustrate you, then ask why they upset you. Flip those answers and you have some of your values. For instance, if you get upset when waiting in a line for a long time, you may think that whoever is responsible is inefficient and inconsiderate. Okay, now flip "inefficient" and "inconsiderate" to their opposites and you can see how efficiency and politeness may well be two of your values.

EXERCISE 2: HEROES

Think of someone you admire. What kind of person did that person have to be to accomplish what they did? The answer will point toward more values. Perhaps you'll choose a relative who continually took risks in business. So, risk might be one of your values.

EXERCISE 3: FIRE!

Imagine coming home to find your house is ablaze. The fire chief says that your family and pets are safe and that there is time for you to rush in to save only one thing. What would you rescue and why? If you chose your photo album because the pictures inside were of your family and friends, one of your values might be the value of belonging or feeling connected.

EXERCISE 4: STORY TIME

Reflect on three to five specific stories from your life that are about your accomplishments where:

- You freely chose to pursue them.
- You felt real joy or satisfaction in doing them.
- You were pleased with the results.

These occasions can be drawn from any age and from your personal as well as professional activities. If you have a hard time coming up with any stories, try dividing your life into five-year segments and searching each one for events that work. Or ask someone who knew you at different times in your life for some feedback. The idea is to come up with accomplishments that are significant to you, not ones that might impress somebody else. Once you have identified your stories, ask yourself the following questions:

- Why did you want to do this in the first place?
- Why were you happy while you were doing it?
- Why are you glad you did it?

Your responses to these questions should speak to your values. Good responses go beyond the obvious ones. We often say that a person or a thing makes us happy, but people and things aren't values; they inspire them. If you say someone or something made you interested, excited or happy, then look beyond the physical and see why you were interested, excited or happy. For instance, if you did something for the money, go further and ask why the money was important. Did it spark the feelings—the values—of security? Freedom? Status? Keep asking "Why?"and dig until you find words that touch you inside. When you do, you'll discover what you will need in any situation to be happy.

EXERCISE 5: THE JOB FROM HELL

Make a list of at least 10 elements of a job that you would just hate. Think about work you've done in the past or work you've avoided that just wasn't right, and jot down a word or phrase describing the problem. For example, maybe you once had a boss who micro-managed you all the time, and that drove you nuts. Okay, write "A micro-managing boss."

Once you have your list, create another one next to it that lists the exact opposite things. So, if you wrote, "A micro-managing boss" in your first list, you could write, "A boss that gives me a lot of autonomy and trusts me" in the second list. It's that second list that will point out what is important to you not just at work, but probably in other parts of your life, too. And again, notice that things or people—like a cool boss—point to your core values. Autonomy and trust are values you would probably want no matter where you were, what you were doing, or whom you were with.

Values worksheet

As you go through the previous exercises, you may start to notice certain values showing up more than once. That's good; note them. On the following page is a list of some of the more common ones. Decide what each word means to you. Use them if they seem appropriate and/or use your own. Create a list of from 5 to 10 powerful values, ones that really matter to you.

VALUES WORKSHEET

___ Acceptance   ___ Achievement   ___ Adventure

___ Appreciation   ___ Balance   ___ Belonging

___ Choice   ___ Clarity   ___ Collaboration

___ Commitment   ___ Competence   ___ Competition

___ Completion   ___ Confidence   ___ Connection

___ Contribution   ___ Control   ___ Cooperation

___ Creativity   ___ Discipline   ___ Efficiency

___ Enthusiasm   ___ Excellence   ___ Expression

___ Focus   ___ Freedom   ___ Harmony

___ Honesty   ___ Humor   ___ Imagination

___ Independence   ___ Innovation   ___ Integrity

___ Interaction   ___ Learning   ___ Loyalty

___ Mastery   ___ Meaning   ___ Openness

___ Participation   ___ Play   ___ Progress

___ Recognition   ___ Relationship   ___ Responsibility

___ Reflection   ___ Respect   ___ Risk

___ Safety   ___ Security   ___ Sharing

___ Significance   ___ Solitude   ___ Status

___ Support   ___ Trust   ___ Variety

Appendix E: Instructions for Plotting Your Purpose

Let's play "what if." What if your purpose is to go east, and you are starting out from Los Angeles? One thing you could do is to create a "going east" goal like visiting Chicago. And let's say you went there. After you arrived, would there be more east to go? Sure, you could go to New York. But, is there still more east after New York? Of course, and so you could continue from there, if you liked.

> "The greatest thing in this world is not so much where we stand, as in what direction we are going."
>
> - Goethe

Your life purpose is a lot like heading eastward. It's a choice about the direction towards which you want your life to go. That's one reason why your purpose isn't a goal: You can achieve a goal, but a purpose is pure direction and can only be followed. But your purpose does help you to create good goals. Since it is a direction towards which you move, you can set goals that are in alignment with it.

The value in plotting your purpose is fourfold:

- When you know your purpose and your values, you know what gives your life direction and energy, what gives your life meaning.
- A purpose helps you create goals for the important parts of your life. Goals about career, relationships, money, health and more can all be influenced by your purpose.
- Knowing your purpose will help you make smarter choices because you can make them in alignment with your direction. As a result, you will care more about them. And knowing your purpose will help you bring into your life the kinds of activities, responsibilities and people that will move you forward, and say "no" to those that don't. As

a result, you stay focused, energized and surrounded by supportive people.

- Reminding yourself of your purpose can help to encourage and energize you when things aren't going as well as you like. It can help you to keep moving forward. Even when you are too weak to make any progress, you'll at least know which direction you want to be facing.

Your purpose is determined, in large part, by the impact you want to have in the world. Here are some exercises to help you get some clarity about that impact:

EXERCISE 1: BE CURIOUS

Ask at least five people in your life how you have affected their lives for the better. Try a version of one of these questions:

- How have I affected your life for the better?
- What positive impact have I had in your life?
- How has knowing me made a good difference for you in your life?
- How is your life different in a positive way for knowing me?

When you are done, then ask them how the world is or will be changed for the better—however much—for your having been here. Chances are that when you ask these questions the people you are talking with will start by saying how wonderful you are. That's fine. Soak it in! But remember that what you are actually asking them is how you are impacting them and the world for the better. That is what you need to find out. Be sure to bring the conversation back to that and record their answers.

EXERCISE 2: THE ADMIRER

Think of someone you admire: a person you know now, or have known. Perhaps it's a former teacher, a sports idol, friend or a business leader. You can also identify a character from mythology, or a comic book, or the movies. Anyone you look up to in some way. Then, recall and record the impact they've had both on you and on others.

EXERCISE 3: YOUR IMPACT

Review the stories from the Story Time exercise in the Values-Spotting appendix above. Were any other people involved in those stories? If so, what was your effect on them? How did you impact or influence them for the better? If any of your stories didn't involve other people, try and think of some that did and then answer the above questions again for them.

EXERCISE 4: YOUR LEGACY

Imagine that some relatives of yours two generations from now are paging through a family photo album. They turn the page and there are some pictures of you. They begin to talk about you. It's well known what kind of person you were and the impact you had in your time. What will they say about you? What will be your legacy?

EXERCISE 5: THE GATHERING

This exercise takes place in your imagination and on a piece of paper. Imagine gathering together several groups of people. As you create each group, you may want to list their names on the paper. These people can be alive or not. The first group consists of three to five people whom you have strong and positive feelings toward. The second group is three to five people whom you like, but don't feel strongly about. The third group consists of three to five people whom you recognize from your life, but whom you don't really know. People like your bank teller or mail carrier. And finally, think of just one person for whom you have strong negative feelings of any kind.

Now, in your imagination, bring these people together in one spot, like your living room, a conference room or a park—anywhere you like. In this scenario, they all know that they have been called together for the reason of hearing you tell them something very important, though they don't know what it is.

Picture them all together, looking at you expectantly. Try and see their faces. They don't know this, but you are about to do something incredible. You are about to miraculously grant something—anything—to all these people. It will be the same thing for each and every one of them and whatever you want for them will take effect immediately. Their lives will be changed forever, and for the better, as a result. What will you grant them? What will you tell them? Play this scene out in your mind and then record your wish.

EXERCISE 6: YOUR STATEMENT

Now, looking at your responses to the previous five exercises, use them as clues as to the kind of impact you want to have in the world. (Remember? That's what your purpose is all about.) Then create a first draft of a purpose statement. Here are some examples:

- I connect people to cool opportunities and each other.
- I am the possibility of compassion, humor and acceptance in the world.
- I stand for dependability and kindness in my relationships.
- I am the song that opens the heart to what is and can be.
- I am the wise and kindly lion, protecting the weakest from harm.

Notice that these purposes can easily inspire goals and activities, plus give real direction to someone's life. The final two are metaphors, which for some people can be very inspiring. I once coached an attorney with a local school system who came to me to improve her leadership and communication skills. When Suzanne went through the process of crafting her purpose statement, she was surprised. It read: I am a lively invitation calling everyone to joy, fulfillment and fun! In time, as we continued working together, she ended up leaving her law work to start a company that makes—invitations! She now creates and sells them for weddings, parties and other personal and corporate special events.

To create a life purpose using a metaphor, again, discover what the key impact is that you want to have in the world. Then decide what thing represents that to you. In Suzanne's case, the impact she wanted was for people to have delightful experiences, and she associated that with inviting them to do just that.

I encourage you to create both metaphor and non-metaphor versions to see which is more "you." Experiment with different words and phrases. Use a thesaurus. You can even get a friend involved to help you craft the combination of words that really works for you. Write and rewrite until you create the statement that really fits you and sounds right when you read it aloud (with feeling!). It should engage your imagination, and give you a direction towards which you really want to move.

Finally, your life purpose statement should be short: a sentence of no more than twelve or fifteen words. It should be something you can pull from memory at a moment's notice. An idea that is really part of you. Your internal compass.

The Author: Dan Kennedy

Photo Credit: Yuen Lui Photography Studio

Dan Kennedy has been a professional coach for nearly 20 years. He helped found the Puget Sound Chapter of the International Coach Federation which has grown to become ICF Washington State. He was one of the first coaches to be certified by the ICF in the Pacific Northwest. He has completed The Coaches Training Institute's core curriculum plus their Co-Active® Leadership program and has taught coaching as a leadership skill for various organizations including the University of Washington and at Bellevue College near Seattle.

As a coach, Dan has been featured in the Seattle Times and cited in publications including Inc. Magazine. His coaching clients have included a wide variety of professionals as well as various organizations including Adobe Systems, Campbell Soup Company and the City of Seattle. He has published several articles on coaching and is the author of *Creating Results That Matter: A Coaching Manual for Anyone.* You can reach Dan at (206) 783-6829 and online at Dan@ResultsThatMatter.com.

44296687R00039

Made in the USA
San Bernardino, CA
11 January 2017